BUILD YOUR PROFITS
Second Edition

A BUSINESS GUIDE FOR TRADIES

By Donna Stone

National Library of Australia Cataloguing-in-publication entry:

Title: Build Your Profits
              - A Business Guide for Tradies
              - Second Edition

Author: Donna Stone and guest writer Fionna Reid

ISBN: 978-0-359-67658-3

Notes: Includes index

Subjects: Tips for tradespeople on business

Dewey No.:   658.022

Table of Contents

Disclaimer

All care has been taken in compiling the contents of this book, but no guarantees are given in relation to its accuracy. This book represents the opinions of the author only. The information in this book has been obtained by the author solely from her own experiences as a coach and business consultant and is provided as general information only.

No reader should rely solely on the information contained in this publication as it does not purport to be comprehensive or to render specific advice. As such it is not intended for use as a source of investment or business advice. All readers are advised to retain competent counsel from legal and accounting advisers to determine their own specific business needs.

The author and publisher expressly disclaim all and any liability to any person, whether or not the purchaser of this publication, in respect of anything and of the consequences of anything done or omitted to be done by any such person in reliance, whether whole or partial, upon the whole or any part of the contents of this publication.

Important Notice

Substantial changes are occurring regarding Security of Payment and the Building Industry Fairness (BIF) Act 2017. The 'lawyer tips' were written before these new rules came into place, so I strongly recommend you either contact Fionna Reid directly for the most current status of the Act. Alternatively, you can visit the QBCC website https://www.qbcc.qld.gov.au/blog/legislation/commencement-new-security-payment-laws. Be sure to familiarise yourself with the new rules as I believe timing of action is very critical.

Dedication

This book is dedicated to all the wonderful people in my life, including:

My three sons – Matt, Dan & Nathan

All my exceptional clients – my business would not exist without you.

Donna

My passion is your potential

Introduction

Being great at your trade is critical, but why do some builders and tradies seem to do really well and others ... well, they simply scrape by and really never achieve that level of financial success? Personally, I don't believe it's to do with intelligence or formal education or luck for that matter. What I believe makes the successful and business victorious builder or tradie is that they realise they are not only great at what they do but they endeavour to be great at business. You don't have to be a University graduate or come from a wealthy family to do well in business. It's about your attitude to working hard (and smart) on your business. I'm not talking only about "working on the tools". A good business owner also needs to focus ON the business. You need to work on (or have someone working on) your marketing, your sales, customer service, delivery and ensuring your team are working to their optimum.

To best explain, let's just get started and work through the 75+ tips in this book.

So what gives me the right (or ability) to share my tips with you?

First, before we start, you are probably wondering why this *bird* thinks she can tell me how to succeed in what is traditionally a male industry? I'm in no way new to the building industry, let me assure you.

I was first exposed to the industry through my Dad, who had been in the building game for my entire life. I can remember frequent Saturday mornings that he would take me and my little brother to work at the construction site (well the office, not the actual site, that would breach WH&S). As kids, we are sponges; I would hear discussions and stories about what was going on. Later as an adult, I married a tradie and was directly involved in his business for over a decade helping him go from strength to strength.

Then of course, through my exposure to the industry, many of my clients have been tradies. I've helped small builders, medium sized builders and developers, carpenters, brickies, concreters, earthworks, truckers, plasterers, plumbers, painters, tilers, electricians, scaffolders ... the list goes on and on. Additionally, I have worked with associated industries, ranging from Architects, Civil Engineers and WH&S Consultants.

In fact, about one third of my clients are from the Building & Construction industry. As of this date, all three sons have worked in the trades ... so you can see I've always been heavily involved in the industry.

Knowing the industry is one thing, I also have a background in Accounting, Training and business management and coaching - 30 years' experience in helping Australian businesses – in all industries.

So, this book is about sharing those experiences and knowledge with you – because quite honestly (besides selling books) I really want you to succeed. I believe the building industry is one of the backbones of our country – you guys (and gals) work damn hard – you deserve to not only win – but have some massive victories!

Donna Stone – December 2019.

P.S. Throughout, for ease, I've often said he or she. I believe it makes reading easier than "he or she" or "s/he". I am not being gender specific. No inference or offense is intended.

About the Author

Donna Stone has been helping Australian businesses for more than 30 years. She has been a business coach for over ten years with more than a third of her clients being in the building and construction industry. She has run Employment Agencies, founded, grown and sold successful businesses and worked in top legal and accounting firms. Whilst she does have formal qualifications in Accounting, Training and Business Management, it's the years and years of real world experience that has made her into the industry expert she is today.

Donna currently has professional Memberships with:

- Australian Institute of Management
  - member over 25 years
- International Institute of Directors & Managers
- Institute of Learning Professionals
- Institute of Public Accountants
- Redland City Chamber of Commerce
- Australian Society of Authors
- Queensland Writers Centre
- Redlands Creative Alliance Inc.
- My Networking Group

In addition, she has won dozens of business awards at both local and National level. She is involved in a number of business networking groups at leadership level. Donna is also an international speaker.

Donna has published several books, dozens of e-books, as well as writing hundreds of articles for other sites and magazines. She also ghost writes for other business owners, helping them produce great content, blogs, e-books and books.

Donna raised three sons, who are now all successful young men in their own rights, and does find (some) time for sport, hobbies, art (check out www.artwork2love.com), as well as enjoying beautiful Queensland where she resides.

Guest Writer – Legal Tips

Fionna C. Aitchison Reid LLB, BBSc Director
Aitchison Reid, Building and Construction Lawyers

"I have years of experience successfully helping clients with their building and construction disputes. But I wanted to do more. So at Aitchison Reid, we take our lessons learned from previous disputes and use them to help subbies, trade contractors and building owners avoid disputes and reduce their losses. I am passionate about helping clients and solving issues for them before they become big problems."

Fionna has been a construction lawyer since 2002, and has primarily worked for subcontractors, trade contractors and owners.

Aitchison Reid was established in 2012. The building and construction law practice currently has a team of five and provides both pre contract advice and helps clients with their disputes (litigation). Aitchison Reid is a Master Plumbers Association Queensland law practice and provides advice to its trade members.

In 2015, Fionna co-founded the Women in Building and Construction Group with her colleague Lynne Sturgess. The group provides support to women from all parts of the construction industry and meets on a bi-monthly basis.

Fionna was the first person to complete co-joint Building Science and Law degrees in New Zealand in 1999 and was a NAWIC award winner in 2016.

Fionna is constantly involved in proactively educating the industry and has spoken at events hosted by MPAQ, NAWIC and Aitchison Reid.

My Special Request to You

If you have enjoyed this book and have found some valuable tips in it, I would be more than happy for you to share the word. However, rather than simply forwarding it to your associate or friend, I would really appreciate you giving their email address to me (or you giving them mine) so that we can add them to the database. This means that as new books are released, then we are able to alert them directly and keep them informed.

Secondly, if you did enjoy this book, I always value testimonials – even just a couple of quick lines in an email … that would be greatly appreciated. If you have any suggestions or requests on related topics you are particularly interested in, do let me know via email to: donna@donna-stone.com.au.

Please also like my business pages on social media and check out the websites:

Authoring:

https://www.facebook.com/DonnaStoneAuthoring

or

www.donna-stone.com.au

Testimonials for Donna Stone

Author & Coach

Wow Donna! I thought you did a great job with your first book. Who'd have thought you could cram so much more into another book? You've really hit the bases. This is a great handbook for anyone wanting to grow their business. Congratulations! **Rob Lovett - Elite Carpet Dry Cleaning**

We have been provided with practical, clear advice and prompt friendly service. We have been assigned one bookkeeper who we are able to contact directly and who knows our accounts and understands our business therefore being able to provide quick, accurate information when necessary. We also had cause to request additional material and data from our accounts and found the assistance and report presented to be not only helpful but also valuable to our business. Donna Stone has provided us with a prompt and professional service and we are happy to recommend her. (Re Stone Consulting).
Aaron Denovan, General Manager - Roturn Engineering

Donna Stone has benefited our company immensely. The advice and support that she has given us has allowed the business to run more smoothly and effectively. I would highly recommend her for her efficient and personal service.
Liona Constructions - Brisbane QLD

Donna has done more in a few weeks than several other coaches have done in several months; WOW I was amazed at how personalized and to the point Donna's methods were. I would encourage anybody who is looking to move on in business to contact Donna, you will not be disappointed.
David Ibell – Grass Action Mowing, Brisbane, QLD

Donna Stone has helped us with our business so much, that I highly recommend her to anybody and have done so over the past couple of years. I find that because she knows the construction industry so well, it really helps her to understand our company needs. **Klenner Electrical - Redland City**

Donna bridges the gap between theory and reality in small businesses today. Steps that can be used right now with immediate results. A must read for every small business owner.
Jon Hui, Owner/Manager - Bank of Queensland, Manly, QLD

Donna Stone is a highly professional business woman and qualified trainer whose services have been invaluable to this business.
Greg Thornton Constructions - Kenmore, QLD

Little concern or care is afforded in small business as it intertwines its way through the mire of everyday business, especially through difficult times. As someone with extensive experience I have seen some close down, some go bankrupt and many struggle along. This sensible and practical, in the hand, book of advice is based on a wealth of qualified experience and is engaging to all its readers. **Adelia Berridge - Style Wise Furnishings Pty Ltd**

You've benefited our company immensely! The advice and support has allowed the business to run more smoothly and effectively.
Luis & Fiona Marcon - Builders, Redland City, QLD

Donna Stone's skills are of a very high standard; her manner very "switched on".
L&M Concreting - Manly

As small business owners we juggle many roles and are usually time poor. This can be very frustrating and sometimes makes you wonder why you went into business in the first place. "I thought this working for myself gig was meant to give me freedom" ... lol. I engaged Donna Stone's services to not only give us more direction but also help us put together a short and long-term business plan. Donna is that little person that sits on your shoulder and reminds you to keep on task. We have found her advice to be spot on and it's definitely like having another set of eyes that help you see a lot clearer. I was once told that a business is not a business until you can walk away from it and it runs itself otherwise you are just self-employed. The same person advised me to get a business coach and I'm glad I listened. Thanks Donna, you are making a big difference in fine-tuning our great brand. **Tony Mora – Suncoast Outdoor Living**

As a Business Coach, Donna is very good in helping you find direction, set goals and my favourite, make you accountable! Donna has helped us implement procedures that have streamlined our business and has taken a lot of the pain and worry out of a running a business. I highly recommend her to anyone wanting to get on top of things and take their business to the next level.
Sarah Brereton - Floworks Plumbing, Redland Bay / Redland City

---

Getting Setup Right

1 Starting Out with the Right Business Structure
GETTING SETUP RIGHT

Yes, I'm sure you've heard the word 'structure'. I'm talking in this instance about business structure. How are you setup? There are 4 main structures, and below is a table outlining those four, their main features, the advantages and disadvantages.

ENTITY	ADVANTAGES	DISADVANTAGES
Sole Trader	Cheap and easy to setup and operate. In fact almost no setup required as you are trading in your own name.	No safety regarding asset protection or being sued. No tax benefits
Trust	Relatively cheap to setup, and fairly simple from an accounting perspective. Trusts and companies are the most popular structures.	Doesn't allow profits to remain in the trust. Often most ideal linked with a company.
Company	More secure method, especially linked with a trust. Allows excess profits to be taxed at 30% (or less, as these rates drop).	The most expensive option to setup, and to maintain and profit is not yours; belongs to the company unless drawn down as wages or a loan.
Partnership	Like a trust, fairly easy to setup and in my opinion work best in a husband/wife situation.	Partnerships with other people can be full of peril as often a proper agreement isn't drawn up. Some people, for example, don't realise their partner can incur debt on their behalf.

You don't have to understand every structure, but please do understand YOUR structure. Ensure you have an Accountant that you can talk to, who really understands your business and your objectives. Ask your accountant to explain to you what your structure means and what's important that you do within your structure. Get him/her to give you the rules around your structure. What can you do or not do?

One example is that if you have a company, you cannot simply take the money out of the bank account and use it personally, without allocating it either as a wage (and having tax deducted) or as a loan to the company (meaning you have to pay it back and likely with interest). A lot of builders and tradies get caught by this. They figure, they earned the money, so it's theirs! Not so, the company owns the income, and profits, until it's passed onto you either as a wage, loan or distribution. This can be heavy stuff, so just be aware of these rules. Know what you can safely do.

2 Getting an ABN, Bank Accounts & Insurances
GETTING SETUP RIGHT

Before any of this, we're working on the basis you are a licensed tradesperson already. You have your BSA license or licensing within the relevant body, such as is required for Electricians or Plumbers. I strongly recommend you sort out your licensing before you go any further.

So once you have sorted out your structure, possibly had your accountant purchase a company for you and set it up, then you will need to do a few things. Check first with your accountant, they may be doing this for you.
Alternatively, you can do it yourself (though take care to do it correctly) if you want to save a bit of money. Here are the next steps:

1. Apply for an ABN. Go to www.abn.gov.au. You will need to fill out a lot of answers. If you really are unsure, again, ask your accountant or bookkeeper. If you've recently setup an entity, it's very likely your accountant has already setup your ABN (and even GST registration for you).

2. Apply for GST Registration. This is part of the ABN application. If your turnover (by this I mean your total gross sales) is over $75K (before GST) then you must register for GST. If it's under this threshold, you can still register for GST; it's your choice. You would register for GST voluntarily if you wanted to portray the illusion of size (non GST registered businesses are obviously very small) or perhaps you will register if you are close to the threshold and don't want to stress about keeping a close eye for when you tip over that threshold. However, the negatives are that you have to collect GST for the government, report at least each quarter (usually). If you are competing for consumer work with non GST registered people, they may get the work if they are cheaper due to not charging GST.

    Let me explain this concept. If the job is $100 for both you and a competitor, but he is NOT registered for GST, his price to an individual is $100. You however, as GST registered, need to add GST so your price is $110. Yes, you may not need to add exactly 10% as you'll have input credits, but to keep things simple, I'm suggesting 10%. Someone may simply choose the other person because they are cheaper.

3. The third thing you need to do is open a bank account or two in the business name. I say "or two" because I strongly recommend you have a GST/Savings and Tax/Super account, separate from your operating account. Somewhere you can

park some money for the BAS, tax or super payments. When it's in the same bank account as your operations, this money often gets spent. Remember to open the accounts in the name of the entity; so if it's a company, in the company name, not your personal name.

4. Fourth, you need to look at insurances. Now consider the essentials, such as public liability (remember to request your Certificate of Currency) but also look into income protection and total disability or life insurance. I'm no insurance expert, so get onto an insurance broker who can help you with this. They may charge a small fee, but a good one is worth it (especially when it comes time to make a claim). Remember also WorkCover.

Even if you are not employing, but working for a builder or principal contractor, they may expect you to have a WorkCover (or Workers Compensation) policy regardless of whether you have staff. In Queensland, you can get a minimum level policy for around $400 – even if you are not employing. Remember also with these policies (at least for Queensland) that Directors don't have to be included – unless you want to be. Also for the gross wages, be sure to include any super.

3 Join a Professional Body in your Industry
GETTING SETUP RIGHT

There are absolutely so many professional bodies in the building industry, including:

- Housing Industry Association (HIA)
- Master Painters Association (MPA)
- Master Plumbers Association (MPA)
- Queensland Master Builders Association (QMBA)

This is just a sample; there are so many more. Simply Google your industry such as "Tilers professional association" and see what comes up.

So why join a professional association for your industry?

- Foremost is the relevant education.
- Regular bulletins, newsletters and magazines
- Access to advice and consultation
- Member benefits – eg discounts on fuel or insurances
- Workshop and training day activities, and more.

Remember, if you join an industry body, use it. Read the materials they send you. Make a point of regularly attending at least one of their workshops every few months.   You can't go to them all (you likely won't have the time) but do review each one and pick the ones which you really believe will benefit you and your business.

4 Get a Bookkeeper
GETTING SETUP RIGHT

Unless your trade is bookkeeping, then get a professional bookkeeper to do the day to day bookkeeping for your business. This isn't just a plug for bookkeepers, but about you delegating to someone who will do it better and quicker than you. Understand you cannot be an expert in everything. You are great at what you do, but don't expect to be an expert in accounting, legal, bookkeeping, administration, industry relations and more. Find the experts, gurus and consultants in these fields.

I'd owned bookkeeping businesses for over 15 years and so often I heard the excuses why someone thinks they don't need a professional bookkeeper, things like:

"It's not that hard, I can do it myself."

"Bookkeeping isn't important, I won't worry about it.'

"I can't afford to pay someone to do it."

"I know my bookkeeping isn't right – but doing the work is more important."

I understand where these phrases come from, you are low on money, think earning money is more important and really, don't see the importance or value in paying to get it done. But that's false.

Firstly, I'm talking about GOOD services – not cheap or dodgy services, but ones from professionals who know their stuff.

Let me give you a couple of reasons to consider these services:

- One brickie business who came on board with us, started getting us to do up his client invoices. He was incredibly busy, but he wasn't able to pay the boys, almost went bust because his cash had dried up due to non-invoicing. Being busy is great, but don't lose focus of the cash flow.

- Another business, commercial concreters were able to keep their cash flow going. They were about to over pay their instalment tax by $78K on the BAS. Because we showed initiative and varied the instalments down to a level which was almost spot on with what needed to be paid, he didn't overpay the ATO. The correct amount of instalment tax was paid, the ATO were satisfied, and the business had extra cash.

- And probably the best story is an accountant who took over lodging the tax returns for the business. The owner had lodged the previous year. The accountant reviewed that prior year and found some serious errors – in the favour of the Tax Office. After revising, the builder got back just over $100,000. Totally legitimate!

Of course too, your bookkeeper can help you setup your accounting program, whether you decide to use MYOB, Xero, Cashflow Manager, Quickbooks or something else. Please have a quality bookkeeper or accounting program consultant setup your data file. Remember this, if the foundations are not solid, what you build on that will not be solid either – it's the same as house construction – foundations are really important.

5 Educate Yourself
GETTING SETUP RIGHT

Educate yourself – read articles on business subjects, attend seminars and gain knowledge. Sometimes it is not only about learning something new, but refreshing ourselves with reminders on what we should be doing – and then **do it.** Constant self-improvement will equate to business improvement.

6 Setup a Website
GETTING SETUP RIGHT

Let's face it, today if someone is looking for something they mostly just Google it. Whether it's a pizza, a pool or a plumber, Google is where everyone is looking. Sure, people (especially those who are older) will look at the local newspaper for "Trade Services" but unless you want only an aged clientele, then you need to get with the times and get a website setup. Here I would suggest you don't go the cheapest at $200. You get what you pay for. However you don't need to spend more than $2,000 for a simple site either. Remember that once you setup a website, you also have to engage someone to do Search Engine Optimisation (SEO). If you are stuck on either of these, just contact me; I know some really good people in both fields.

Consider having on your website a quick "get a quote" button, which can be simply you calling them, or a more complicate questionnaire where they put in info to actually get an estimate via the website. Just remember whatever the method, don't overcomplicate things – make it easy to use.

7 Start an Asset Register for your Tools!
GETTING SETUP RIGHT

Even with a simple Excel spreadsheet start keeping track of your assets – your accountant will need this when he goes to do your tax, so make it easy for him. The fields you will need are:

- Date acquired
- Price paid (ex GST if you are registered and claimed the GST)
- Tool description including model number
- Serial number (very handy for your insurance broker, especially if you need to make a claim)

Keeping a list of your assets means that depreciation can be calculated correctly; and depreciation is an expense for your business which will reduce your taxable income – which means less tax! Additionally you may want to include in this spreadsheet dates of last service, or when 'test and tagging' is required.

8 Get a Coach!
GETTING SETUP RIGHT

Some business owners or operators think only failing businesses need a business coach. This is wrong. If your business has room for improvement or an increase in success – then there is room for a business coach. A business coach works for anyone who is dedicated to their business. So honestly, if you are not going to follow their advice, do their homework or action their guidance, then business coaching is a waste of money.

BUT, do the work, follow the plan, action the homework and I can assure you, you will see results. The business coach will pay for him/herself ten-fold. The benefits of a business coach include:

- Improved sales and profit from having someone knowledgeable guide and show you how
- Help you get setup – step by step
- They will help you with staff – valuable pointers
- They will help you re-discover your passion, give you back that motivation and drive
- They will help you find clarity – what's important to you
- They will help you define your goals and aims
- They will help you focus – how to achieve those goals – the actual steps you need to take
- They will link you to information or sources. If you need a great accountant, I'll bet they could refer one to you.
- They will help you navigate changes in the economy and market place
- They will provide a second opinion
- Best of all, they will be someone you are accountable to. They will demand results, push you, prod you and yes, when you achieve, congratulate you

I am myself a business coach, but also know others in the industry if I am not able to take you on … simply just contact me via my website www.donna-stone.com.au and we can discuss what you need.

9 Set some Goals

GETTING SETUP RIGHT

"Businesses don't plan to fail, they fail to plan".

A pretty simple statement and no doubt those of us who have been around awhile have heard this many times. Yet, how many of us really plan properly?

Do you plan your day?

Do you plan your week?

Do you plan the next 90 days?

Have you written down your goals for the year?

So if I asked you the question "where do you want to be in ten years' time", do you know? Maybe you have a certain desire which isn't specific? It may be something like:

"I want to have a great business"

"I want to be a rich"

"I want to be successful".

Great, but these goals are not specific and are vague at best. How do you determine what a successful business is? What is rich? I bet I could ask 20 people to put a dollar value to the term "rich" and I would get close to 20 different answers.

So here is what I suggest – write up a goal sheet. Break it up into time zones:

- Goals to be achieved within 3-12 months
- Goals to be achieved within 5 years
- Goals to be achieved by retirement

Determine your goals and then determine which time zone they fit into. Now the important thing here is to **write it down!** I cannot stress that enough. Thinking is good, but putting those thoughts onto paper is the first step to achieving those goals.

So you have set your goals. Now is the hard part. How will you achieve those goals? Maybe one of your goals was to save for a deposit on a house? Perhaps the activity to work towards that goal is to put $100 a week aside in a savings account; or better yet, set up an automatic sweep to that savings account. There may be three or four strategies or activities for each of those goals.

So, do you see where I am coming from here? You set your goals and then *plan* how you will achieve those goals. Think of this like travelling to a destination. You determine where you want to go. Plan how you will get there. Take this street; turn right at that road, etc.

10 What about Franchising?
GETTING SETUP RIGHT

Franchising is a great concept for many businesses. If you are happy to follow a proven, tried and tested system that semi guarantees success, then it's for you. You are buying into the name, the branding and of course all the systems and processes. As a franchisee you don't have to re-invent the wheel or start from scratch. To develop a business can take years; this is definitely a way to turbo kick start that process.

Many people think of food outlets when thinking about franchising, but they make up only about 16-17% of Australian franchises. There is everything from accounting, gardening, cleaning, pet stores and so much more. A franchise really can be very diverse.

Franchising began in Australia in the early 1970's under the influence of US franchises. Fast food systems such as McDonalds, Pizza Hut and KFC. It has revolutionized retail in Australia.

However, some franchises arrangements are 'tough' to say the least and can make it extremely hard for you to make money, let alone break even. I strongly recommend you read the proposed agreement BEFORE even paying any deposits or show any commitment. I have seen some scary agreements. If after reading it, you like what you see and wish to proceed, absolutely be sure to have a solicitor go through it with you. These documents are usually written FOR the franchisor, so will be usually written to benefit them.

Money Matters

11 Invoice!
MONEY MATTERS

You may have heard "cash is king" … well I believe "cash is the whole royal family!" The first step of getting your cash flowing is by invoicing. This might seem obvious, but I've seen far too often business struggling on a cash flow level and the reason behind it has started with not invoicing or slow invoicing.

Firstly, you must have a system in place for your invoicing. I heard of one business that went to their accountant asking why they had no money but seemed to be doing well. Turns out, after investigation, the accountant discovered that about 3 months ago, they had not invoiced one whole month. The flow through didn't occur till several weeks later. You need to ensure things do not get overlooked, whether it be a whole month, or an on-charge of a stove or hot water system. If you are unsure of a system to use, again your bookkeeper or accountant can help you. It might be that when the purchases come in you write on it "TO INVOICE JOB # 437" and the bill cannot be entered, paid or filed until the invoice is done and it's written "invoiced 15/7 # 4522". Sometimes the simplest systems are the best.

Then of course there are those which really struggle with invoicing regularly. Waiting until you have no money to pay the boys wages on Friday is NOT an option. Most trades should invoice at least on a weekly basis. Set time aside as invoice day. A lot of tradies I know simply finish work at lunchtime, let the boys finish up and then go home to spend an hour or two invoicing. Alternatively when the info comes in, they put the invoice info in their bookkeepers' tray and she does up the invoices each week or fortnight when she visits.

Remember these 4 pointers:

- The longer you let it go, the more likely something gets forgotten
- The sooner you invoice, the sooner it can be paid
- If you leave it too long, people leave, move away, go bankrupt and you miss out
- The more you put it off, the bigger the job becomes and the more you'll dread it.

12 ASK to be Paid!
MONEY MATTERS

An official survey, found that 25% of businesses did NOT ask to be paid! One in four businesses simply never rung up and said "please pay my bill". The thing is, there are businesses out there that bank on this. I had one client who told me one day, "Donna, I only pay you when you start screaming". She had a very slow payment history, and although I knew she was "good for it" I couldn't understand why she always left it till so late. Of course, after this, I started "screaming" a lot sooner. I know some businesses which simply pay no-one until they ring up and ask. That means they pay only 3 out of 4 bills and basically "get off" paying that 25% of those who don't ring.

Please – don't be one of those 25%. Here's the process in simple terms:

- As people pay you, record the payment.

- Review the list of what's owing every WEEK.

- Ring those unpaid and ask politely for payment.

- Write down any promises of payments (including date they promised, what they promised and who you spoke to).

- If the promise didn't eventuate ring AGAIN. Remind them that last Thursday they promised to pay $XXX by Tuesday and you've checked the account and it's not in yet. Get a stronger commitment from them and if worse comes to worse, don't be afraid to use a Collection Agency.

- Have a set day for calling to be paid. Do it every week and again, if you don't have time, delegate it to a suitable person, but remember this – **"Honey gets more flies than vinegar"**. The best collection results are by someone who is nice but firm – the rude, abrasive or abusive collector won't have as good results and will lose clients and customers.

Lawyer's Tip

If you are undertaking construction work, or supplying materials or related services to the construction industry, you may be able to use your State's legislation (Acts) on payment claims to help enforce payment (Security for Payment) legislation.

Each State has a different Security for Payment Act and each Act has different requirements. It is best to contact a construction lawyer in your State to find out how to use the Act to your benefit.

Although the Acts are all different, the purpose of the Acts is to provide a process for industry members to enforce payment quickly and to separate unpaid debts from disputes. Unpaid debts are treated as debts due and are enforceable in Court, while disputes can be sent to adjudication for fast track resolution. If used properly the Security for Payment legislation can give your debt collection arsenal real power.

13 Charge a Quote Fee
MONEY MATTERS

I know with a few established tradies, they are over the whole quoting scene. People will ring up to get 3 quotes to change a light bulb. It's silly. In that case, you may choose to give an estimate over the phone (subject to inspection before you start the job). One strategy I know one experienced tradie does is that he charges a fee to quote. If he's successful in his quote, this fee comes off the price of the job. He now knows that anyone who pays for the quote is serious about getting the job done and are not getting a million quotes for a small job. A warning though, this isn't common practice, so not to be done by those new to business – some customers won't get on board, regardless of how genuine their enquiry is.

14 Formalise your Variations
MONEY MATTERS

You may think that tracking variations is a waste of time – they don't add up to much. Let me assure you that is not the case. I worked for a builder who thought this, but after being convinced to start using a Variation Book, after a year he was absolutely flabbergasted by the value of the variations. They really do add up.

Again, this can be a simple process. Get a Variation carbonised book from QMBA or HIA. When a client says to you they want to change something or add an extra metre here or extra cupboard there, take a moment to write up a variation sheet.

Consider your extra cost of the variations and then write up the variation and see your customer. Don't forget to add extra time this will require, so that your contracted end date can be extended if needed. Even if you don't need that extra time now, you may later, so don't skip utilising that option. Have them sign the variation accepting the additional cost.

Lawyer's Tip

Just like the name suggests a variation is a change to the terms of your contract. A variation should be treated with as much importance as your contract.

Variations are often the cause of disputes between parties, so there is even more reason to make sure that your variations are in writing.

As a minimum, variations should include a description of the change, whether and by how much the change is going to affect the timing of the project and/or the cost. If you are not sure how to cost the variation, you should set out how you will calculate it.

Please note you will need to comply with the terms of your contract relating to variations and even if there are no terms in your contract, you may be required by law to provide a variation document. Some States also require that you to provide certain information in the variation document to comply with your licensing; make sure to check with your licensing provider and/or a local construction lawyer.

15 Invoice Variations Straight Away!
MONEY MATTERS

Many builders and tradies tend to leave the variations until the final invoice. I suggest you don't. As soon as the varied work is done, give them an invoice for this. Enclose a copy (ensure you keep the original) of the signed variation. With the copy of what they have signed, they have no reason (as long as the job was done well) to not pay the bill promptly.

If you leave all the variations until the last and final bill, not only have you delayed invoice (and affected your cash flow) but it's often this final invoice is the one which is disputed. People will keep paying you to keep the work happening, but it's at the final payment that if there is a dispute, they will hold that final payment. It might just be something super simple, like some clean-up or something cosmetic, but people figure that once they've handed over the final payment, they have nothing to barter with you to get things finished up the way they want. The variation might not be disputed, but it gets caught up with the final payments. And let's face it, sometimes people don't have a great budget for their work … they go over budget and oops, they've run out of money to finish paying you. If you invoice variations early on, you'll get wind of any financial issues early in the piece; you can even suspend work until payments occur, but once the job is finished, you're not in a strong position.

16 Make it easy for people to pay you!
MONEY MATTERS

Make it as easy as possible to get paid; ensure your invoice has all payment methods (including your bank account details, BPAY reference number or address where cheques are mailed). Even better pay the low $20 a month rental fee for a mobile EFTPOS machine. When you finish a job, it's all good – you then offer them to pay cash, credit or EFTPOS. And in fact, to avoid any delays, have this lined up in advance when booking the job. Enquire then, "will you be paying cash, credit or EFTPOS on the day? We do have mobile facilities." That way there is little excuse. As soon as you walk away from a job, without payment in hand, you increase the possibility of not being paid at all – and certainly give yourself extra work in chasing payment.

17 Implement KPI's
MONEY MATTERS

Ok, this is probably sounding technical – but KPI stands for Key Performance Indicator and they are great tools. You may have very basic KPIs and possibly listed in a spreadsheet broken up by the 12 months. What was your profit at the end of each month? That is a core and simple KPI.

Another good one is Net Profit as a percentage of Sales. Let's say that your sales last month were $285,000 and your net profit (bottom line) was $11,800.

See below:

11800 ÷ 285000 x 1/100.   ANSWER: 4.14%

Some other excellent ratios (usually calculated via a process similar to the above) are:

- Debtors as a % of Sales
- Direct Costs (COGS) as a % of Sales
- Overheads as a % of Sales
- Wages as a % of Sales (and you might want to include super in these figures)

Need more help on KPIs? Email donna@donna-stone.com.au to purchase the eBook.

18 Calculate your Break-evens
MONEY MATTERS

It's important we know our breakeven point. If you are a service business where your main 'product' is hours or you are actually selling products, the process is the same. Let's work through an example. Firstly let me explain a few terms:

Fixed Costs: these are your overhead expenses; expenses that you will have whether you make a sale or not, eg. accounting fees, phones, vehicle insurance and rego, rent, office staff etc.

Variable Costs: these are your costs relating to the sale. They might include direct labour, materials, freight for delivery of stock or salespeople's commissions.

Selling Price: how much to sell the item before **excluding** GST.

The formula is: Fixed costs / (Selling price – Variable costs)

So imagine that we sell an item for $30 with the direct (variable cost) of each item being $10 and that the fixed costs (overheads) are $200 per day.

$$= \$200 / (\$30-\$10)$$
$$= \$200 / \$20$$
$$= 10$$

So this means that we have to sell 10 items per day in order to breakeven. Anything sold over goes towards profit. Now remember that it won't go directly to profit. If in a day you sold 5 units above the 10 breakeven, then the profit would be 5 x ($30-10), or $100.

---

19 Money Cycle
MONEY MATTERS

If you are not working on contract, and essentially issuing invoices and accounts, then it's really important you track how long it's taking to get paid – and more importantly chasing payment. Remember that cash is the 'life blood' of every business. It's a statistical fact that the longer you let a debt go, the greater the likelihood you won't get paid! Here's how to calculate your average collection days:

A = sales for the last 12 months (inc GST, let's use $3,762,000)
B = days in the year (let's use 365)
C = debtors value for the last month (in this example, let's use $270,000

$$\frac{A}{B} = X \quad \text{then} \quad \frac{C}{X} = Y$$

$$\frac{3762000}{365} = 10{,}307 \quad \text{then} \quad \frac{270000}{10307} = 26.2$$

ANSWER: In this scenario, it takes the business on average 26.2 days to collect their debts.

20 Know % leads convert to sale
MONEY MATTERS

Every business should keep a record of where their lead (enquiry for new business) came from. Did your mate John send them over? Was it the architects you did a job for a while ago? You should be tracking these connections for 3 main reasons:

1. To thank the person for the introduction – they are more likely to keep sending business your way if you show a little appreciation. It might be shouting lunch at the pub, or a bottle of wine, or simply a 'thank you' card in the mail.

2. By keeping track of your leads, you can also follow up on them.

3. If you know how you went last month (or last year) you can work at improving your performance.

So, by tracking your leads you know, for example, you had 15 leads this month. If you had 3 new clients, your conversion percentage would equate to 20%. This means of course, if you wanted to get 5 new clients next month, you would need 25 leads! (25 x 20% = 5).

Simple often works best. You might have a notebook, or an excel spreadsheet, or even just a white board in the office, but the trick here is to always ask the person "how did you hear about us?" and WRITE IT DOWN! In the example below, it's just the basic info about the lead, and their phone number, and the source or the person who sent the business your way.

Lead Name	Date Rec'd	Phone No.	Source
Mary Smith	15.8.14	0418 111 222	John @ BCC

21 Know your financial cycles
MONEY MATTERS

The most obvious cycle in the building industry is your 30 day trade accounts. Quite often you get the invoice after the end of the month and have 30 days to pay, which means if you purchased on the 1st of the month, you are getting all that month plus the 30 days to pay – a total of 60 days!

So, it makes sense that if you can control your buying patterns, purchase early in the month, so the job can get paid before you even have to pay for your materials.

22 Get a deposit
MONEY MATTERS

This is so incredibly important if your materials are a good portion of the job. If you are say a cabinet maker, then your outlay for materials is high. Under most contracts you may be stuck with the standard being 5% for deposit. Even try to negotiate the deposit being higher in this case. Certainly if there is no contract, make your deposit at least 30 to 50% or to the legal level your State allows. I have even known some places who charge 100% deposit. That I believe is over the top, and only the most established business could get away with it – or the most unique business who has no competitor.

Lawyer's Tip

It is always useful to have as much money paid to you before you start work as possible, but the size of your deposit may be limited by law. Make sure that you check with your licensing provider and/or a local construction lawyer to make sure that you are charging the correct deposit under the Acts that apply in your State.

Another way of securing payment before you do work is by using an escrow service. An escrow service provides a trust account, in which the owner's money can be held in trust until the work is done. This makes sure that the money exists before you do the work and is secure while you do the work.

23 Have a Contract or Agreement
MONEY MATTERS

Please never assume your customer will do business correctly. It's incredible how many people think they can get away with not paying. So, have contracts and agreements in place to ensure that once you build that amazing deck on the back of their house overlooking their brand new swimming pool – that you get paid, whilst they are enjoying your hard work.

Many businesses, such as curtain and blind stores, actually ask "How are you going to pay for this" and insist you pay on the spot once the job is done. Don't be shy asking for payment.

Lawyer's Tip

A contract doesn't need to be in writing to be binding. The problem is if it is not in writing, it is extremely difficult to prove what has been agreed between the parties. A written contract can also help protect you by having a clear process if something goes wrong. Often contractors "borrow" clauses from their competitors' contracts because the clauses sound "legal" without any understanding of what the clauses mean.

If you don't understand your contract, it is unlikely your team or customers will, and that can cause more confusion, more disputes and more wasted time for you. Your contract should be like any other tool in your tool box; it should work for you, you should understand it and how it works.

To check if you are required to use written building contracts and what information you are require to include, you can check with:

- A local construction lawyer;
- Your local trade association; or
- Your state governing body.

Some local trade associations provide contracts that comply with your State's laws and are personalised to your trade.

24 Have your quote include your T&C's
MONEY MATTERS

An excellent method to provide T&C's (Terms & Conditions – the rules by which you want to do business) is to include your T&C's as part of your quote. Then if your prospective customer wishes to proceed you have them sign the quotation as accepting the quote AND your terms & conditions. It's not as sharp as signing a contract or agreement, but achieves a similar result.

At the end of the day, it's not just about covering your rear legally, but also about being clear and transparent up front. Far better everyone knows the 'deal' and accepts it, than disputes to ensue after the act. Disputes,fighting and legal action (even if you are a winner) are not fun, not productive, waste your time working on your business and are just plain stressful.

And of course – have a Solicitor or Lawyer review your T&C's before you use them – just to ensure all bases are correctly covered. For example, some industries are not allowed to charge interest on outstanding accounts – your Solicitor will know industries affected by these special rules.

Lawyer's Tip

A quote containing terms and conditions is a great way to make sure that the terms that you want form part of your contract. Your terms and conditions must be written with care to make sure:

- You comply with your licensing requirements for that particular type of contract (eg domestic building contracts often have particular requirements);
- You make the most of Security for Payment legislation; and
- Your interests are protected.

It is vital that your contract is compliant with your State's requirements and protects you. You may be able to obtain a compliant contract through:

- Your state governing body (please note these tend to be basic and very general);
- Your local trade association (these contracts are more specialised for your trade);
- A local building and construction lawyer (these contracts can be tailored to your business requirements).

Please remember that the cost of getting good quality legal advice from a building and construction lawyer at the beginning is nothing compared to the consequences of not getting your contracts and business processes right, which can include costly disputes (litigation) and/or fines from your regulator.

25 Watch your expenses
MONEY MATTERS

Ensure you are not paying a fortune in phone services, or bank fees, but don't be silly about it. Remember you "need to spend money to make money". Do not cut costs on things like marketing and advertising as these costs are really investments in your business and critical to its good health.

On the subject of marketing, be sure to track where the leads are coming from, so you know what is working. If the $600 advert in the local paper got no leads, why continue to run it. However, if you got $100,000 worth of work from that $600 advert, you might consider running it again and again!

26 End of Financial Year Activities
MONEY MATTERS

- Contact your accountant regarding tax planning. This is not an activity simply to allow them to bill more; there is actually very good value in this; it's best done BEFORE 30 June however as some strategies cannot be back dated. I am not providing tax advice below; these are prompters to get you thinking about action and a prompter to talk to your accountant. Not everything is suitable for every business.

- If you need to reduce your taxable income, be proactive about this. Ensure your vehicles are serviced in May or June (rather than July or August). Are their tyres getting low? Review your stock of materials, stationery, ink cartridges, stamps, nails, glue, paper and in fact everything you use on a ongoing and regular basis.

- Talk to your accountant or insurance broker about pre paying your insurances.

- If you have rental properties then do they need any work or repairs? (On this note, are you marketing your business in May and June to landlords to get their deductions?).

- Ensure all super (staff and yourself) is in the hands of the super fund by 30 June.

- Don't forget your other obligations like Portable Long Service Leave Certs, WorkCover Policy Renewals, super, BAS and then of course sending all the bookkeeping files to your accountant after 30 June is completed and finalised.

- Finally, remember, it's ideal to keep your debtors clean (debt collect regularly) but if there is anything you have to write off, action those write offs before 30 June.

Lawyer's Tip

Keeping on top of your debtors isn't just great for helping cash flow; it may also help you enforce payment too.

If you are able to use the Security for Payment legislation in your State, there will be options available to you if someone does not pay or raise a dispute (in a payment schedule) such as court proceedings, adjudication and/or suspension of work. However, these options frequently have strict time limits, so if you are too slow taking action you may miss out on being able to enforce your payment claim all together.

Please note we recommend that you find out from a local building and construction lawyer what the time limits are in your State so that you keep them on top of mind when you have a dispute to resolve or an unpaid debt to enforce. Other agencies that are likely to help you are:

- Your State Government Agency; or
- Your local trade association.

27 Job coding AKA Job tracking
MONEY MATTERS

Job coding is simply tracking the income and expenses on each individual job. This is valuable because you want to know when (or when not) you made money on a job and how much. If you know what is working (or not) then you can duplicate (or avoid) that situation in future. For example, your quoting may be off point, or certain costs are blowing out. Remember if you are not making money on a job, why are you getting out of bed?

Many accounting program do job coding very well and your bookkeeper can assist you with this task. Once you setup the job in the system, then it's simply a matter of coding each of your direct expenses to that job. I would not job code things like overhead expenses, accounting, motor vehicle repairs, licenses etc, as these are overhead costs and super hard to allocate across all your current jobs. Only job code costs which relate directly to a job.

28 Do budgets for your business
MONEY MATTERS

I know that when you think of the word 'budget' you think about missing out, or discipline, but instead substitute the term 'profit planning'. Doesn't that sound better!

So, to Profit Plan you need to work out your projected income (be relatively conservative and reasonable about this) and then calculate your business expenses; everything from your materials or overhead costs.

It's always easier to do this when you have historical figures to work on. If you need help in this, contact your bookkeeper, accountant OR visit http://www.donna-stone.com.au/ebooks/ for my e-book on budgeting which goes into good detail.

29 Understanding a simple P&L
MONEY MATTERS

Before I go into calculating overheads, I think I should explain a few basic concepts first. Your first area is turnover which you will find in a P&L (Profit & Loss) Statement. Turnover is essentially your sales – that is the amount you invoice out. Remember, your sales on your P&L Statement, shown from your accounting package, are GST exclusive.

Next you have direct costs. These are often known as COGS (Cost of Goods Sold) or COS (Cost of Sales). These are essentially your direct costs – the costs that you would ONLY have if you have sales. Some examples include materials, direct labour, freight, customs, transport, packaging and costs you are directly reimbursed .

Then you deduct your COGS from sales – you are left with Gross profit. From this you then deduct your overheads. The bottom line is then net profit (before taxes).

So, overheads are those expenses which you incur in running a business – they are not the costs relating specifically to sales, but rather general business costs, like accounting, admin staff, bank fees, subscriptions, memberships and telephones.

MONEY MATTERS

BLOGGS PLUMBING PROFIT STATEMENT
1ST JULY TO 30TH JUNE 20XX

Sales		$450,000
COGS		
- Equipment Hire	$ 10,000	
- Materials	$200,000	
- Subcontractors	$140,000	$350,000
Gross Profit		$100,000
Less Overhead Expenses:		
- Accounting	$ 2,000	
- Bank Fees	$ 1,000	
- Donations	$ 500	
- Interest Paid	$ 500	
- Motor Vehicle Costs	$ 4,000	
- Staff – Office Wage	$25,000	
- Staff – Super (Office)	$ 2,250	
- Staff – Workers Compensation	$ 750	
- Telephone	$ 2,000	$ 38,000
Net Profit		$ 62,000

So in the above situation, when you are costing a job or activity, you know that the items in COGS, such as materials, subbies, equipment hire would be included in the pricing of the job as the direct costs. What many business owners forget is to know what their overhead cost is. In this case the overheads are $38,000 per year.

Image this business works only Monday to Friday (rarely weekends), and always closes for four weeks over Christmas. The business then basically has 240 works days (52 weeks less 4 = 48 weeks x 5 days a week = 240 days). So the daily overhead cost is $158 per day. This means that if only one job is done in a day and a job lasts say three days, then $474 should be added to the quotation calculations to cover these costs; otherwise your job profit is eroded.

31 When profit means a loss
MONEY MATTERS

Still on the subject of overhead costs and pricing, imagine you cost a job as follows (without the overheads) and the job runs for 6 work days:

Materials	$4,000
Staff's Labour (6 days)	$3,000
Profit	$1,000
	$8,000
Add 10% GST	800
	$8,800

So to organise this job you only had to spend three hours, so you figure that was an easy $1,000 – in fact you got over $330 an hour! Pretty cool – you just made an easy grand – or did you? This job ran for 6 days, and your daily overheads cost you $158, so your business overhead costs were $948. So actually you made $52 (divided by 3 hours) or $17/hr. An apprentice or junior probably makes more money than you. Now imagine the scenario where one of your team stuffs up. The job goes an extra day and you have to re-supply some timber for re-cuts. The employee, of course, expects to be paid. So now you have extra costs of $400 – you just lost money.

32 Are single jobs more profitable?
MONEY MATTERS

Again, having run the stats, and having done years of job coding, I've worked out that for the average small builder (where there is no site manager or supervisor) it makes more money doing one job at a time – because:

- You, as the business owner/builder, can focus on one thing at a time, meaning you can ensure the job runs properly and staff are working to capacity and not 'bludging on the job'.

- You can focus on getting the best prices for materials and subcontractors. When you get busy, you just use the same subbies, and they know they have the work, so when they quote (or invoice) they rarely sharpen their pencils and give you the best price. They get complacent. Not being overly busy, and stretched too thin, and you will have the time to get a second quote, or discuss cost effective methods to save.

- You are onsite – and if anything is going wrong, you are there ready to resolve any issues, before it becomes a situation – whether it be a mistake cutting a piece of timber, or a safety issue, you are there and fully supervising.

33 Where did the cash go?
MONEY MATTERS

This is another one I get asked a lot. The client says they've entered in all their income and expenses and the bank reconciliation is done, and it says they made a profit over the last six months of say $100,000. But, they know they have only $5K in the bank. **Where did the cash go?** Ok, putting aside any possible issue of theft, there are a number of possible reasons, but here are the most common top four:

- They've purchased assets. In correct bookkeeping and accounting, these assets are not an expense, in that they will not be allocated or coded to the Profit & Loss statement (P&L). They are actually coded as an asset and therefore go onto the Balance Sheet. (Your Balance Sheet is a listing of what you own, less what you owe; a statement of your equity or business worth.) So, of course the P&L doesn't account for them and indicates a higher level of profit.

- You have vehicle loans or Hire Purchase Payments. Again, like asset purchases, these payments don't go to the P&L statement, but rather against a liability account, still in the balance sheet.

- The business has paid out personal expenses for you. Again these are not business costs, they are personal, so the bookkeeper should NOT be coding them to the P&L. Again, these will get posted to the Balance Sheet.

- You might have invoiced out $100,000, but does that mean you got paid $100,000? Likely not. It might be that of that $100,000 only $35,000 has been received. Yes, you are owned the money, but until you receive it, it's just sitting in your receivables list (in the Balance Sheet) as money due in. A sale does not equate to cash – not by a long shot.

In all the above examples, it's all to do with correct accounting procedure. It can get really complicated, because you are spending money, but it's not showing on your P&L statement, but instead a different financial report. So you look at your P&L and it shows a profit, but you know there is no money in the bank. That's the semi complicated world of finance, but the important thing for you to know is that this does happen, so not to get overly excited when you see a P&L report saying you have a massive profit. Don't get carried away until you see that million dollars IN the bank!

34 Saving for your BAS
MONEY MATTERS

So in the prior tip, we talked about not getting excited until those profits you got are realised and you actually see a good chunk of money in the bank. Well, still be a little cautious. That money you banked, it's not all yours! Sorry – but the fact is that even if you have paid your workers and all your suppliers, there is still a string of possible bills to come up, including:

- GST or payroll withholding tax to be paid on your BAS
- Income Tax – to be paid on the profit of your business
- Superannuation for your staff and workers

Here is what I suggest to account for the above:

- As you pay your wages, you know what the tax you withheld from wages for that week was. Put this money aside in a savings account.

- As you pay your staff wages, put aside their super into that same savings account – so it's away and saved.

- As you get money in (i.e. customers pay your invoices) I suggest you put aside money for your BAS. Now this doesn't need to be exactly 1/11th (working on Australian GST of 10%) because the fact is that you get input credits on bills you pay – your materials and vehicle fuel etc ... so it might equate to say 7 or 8% of sales. Put this amount aside. So if you get a deposit of $15K, put $1100 or $1200 aside then when the money comes into your account.

- And finally, at the end of the month, you look at your profit statement and let's say you made $20K profit. Let's imagine you are operating as a company, so your income tax rate would be 30%. If you work out 30% of $20K – that's $6,000. Now as your tax is done, your accountant is going to claim depreciation and some other allowable deductions, so in fact, you probably won't need to pay $6K, but hey, what about even putting aside $5K? Put this money aside into a term deposit or high interest earning account. If you put too much aside after a year and your tax bill ends up less, how good would that be? Maybe it might mean you can buy that new (but rather expensive tool) or have a good deposit for a new ute. Not too many people complain about saving money, but I sure know lots of people who wish they'd saved more when their tax bills come in. The easiest way to action all this is have a separate 'GST/Tax' account to set aside these funds.

35 Get a mobile Eftpos/Credit card machine
MONEY MATTERS

Welcome to the 21st century. Your tools are no longer just electric drills or drop saws ... here is another tool every smart tradie will have in his ute (but perhaps not rolling around with the other tools in the back).

A mobile eftpos machine for accepting both debit or credit card payments really is the smart way to go. Yes, you will pay a small amount each month for rental and a percentage of the transaction, but what is the price of not having one of these? So, allow approx. $25-35 a month rental and about 2% of the transaction. I personally do not accept Diners or Amex as these are (in my opinion) expensive cards; almost everyone has Visa or MasterCard. You can either on-charge the fee or simply build it into your admin costs. However. if someone 'stiffs' you for $5K or even $500. because you didn't get payment whilst still onsite at completion, then you've lost way more than the small cost to operate the facility.

36 Ditch the wasting of materials
MONEY MATTERS

For some businesses, material wastage is real. A carpenter who has an employee measure the timber wrong and have to throw it out clearly sees the waste – not only the waste timber (if it can't be re-used) but also the time in having to measure and cut it a second time. Ensure you (and your team) just slow down a tad and do things right and make sure your staff are aware of how much waste can cost!

37 Back-charge other trades if suitable
MONEY MATTERS

This is usually done by builders. If a subbie cuts a power line or breaks something, they get the cost of fixing that item taken off their payment. Remember to request this of the builder if another tradie really stuffs up something you've done. Now, you don't want to be the difficult tradie, so only request this when it's a major thing that is going to cost you money. Say you are a painter, you know that the other trades (like the sparkies) are going to mark the walls a little and you'll be called in for 'touch ups' Factor that into your pricing so it doesn't need to be an 'extra' charge or back-charge. Builders don't want to be referees for the small stuff.

Lawyer's Tip

Back charges are frequently an area of dispute so make sure that you document everything in writing. For example, notify the builder or owner in writing immediately of the issue and take time stamped photos of the damage that has been caused. The photo should also be marked up with a description of what you see; this will help remind you at a later date.

Your contract may have specific terms concerning back charges so make sure you comply with them. If your contract is silent about back charges, they should be dealt with like a variation. Variations may be dealt with in your contract so check your contract and comply with it.

Lawyer's Tip Continued

On all occasions make sure your variations are in writing and that you have the builder or owner's written agreement before you undertake any of the repair work. Because this area is notorious for disputes, try and get agreement to the cost of the variation or how you will calculate it before you do the work.

If you have your own subcontractors, the issue of back charges is definitely something that you will want to include in your written subcontract with them.

38 Financial Distress – Avoid Denial
MONEY MATTERS

Financial distress often leads to insolvency and ultimately bankruptcy. Burying your head in the sand or thinking 'it can't happen to me' is frankly foolish. Don't think that bankruptcy doesn't happen to smart, nice or hardworking people. Often it happens to those who really don't 'deserve' it.

It doesn't always have to be something major that occurs, it can be a string of small events - and suddenly you are unable to pay your bills when they fall due – essentially trading insolvent and as time goes on, it gets worse and then the next thing you know, a batch of creditors are threatening to bankrupt you.

This is very important to identify. Both as a company for your own benefit, but also when supplying products or services to others. You should always avoid trading with a suspect insolvent company. Here is a list of the signs and symptoms. Now remember that each one or even a group of them on their own may not mean insolvency, however the more items you can tick, the more likely they are in financial distress.

- Not paying bills when they are due.
- Paying only in part, not the full amount.
- When chased, offering excuses such as "we're busy", "we don't have the invoice" which can be quite legit, however if they are unable to rectify straight away then the problem isn't in fact likely time/organisation but rather they don't have the money.
- Repeated occurrences of the above.
- Your inability to contact them, the person is never available or simply they stop answering the phone.
- The phone is disconnected.
- Of course having cheques dishonoured, bouncing or post-dated is another strong sign.

At this point, if it's a regular occurrence, once you are paid, I would consider either cessation of supply permanently OR making them pre-paid or COD. A random once off can just be nothing ... but be aware and alert.

If you are in distress, please don't ignore it; seeking help early in almost every case I've seen has meant the business was able to go on and trade out of their distress.

39 Save for a rainy day
MONEY MATTERS

Sure, we've all heard it, but how many of you in business have stocked some money away for that time when things just go completely pear-shaped? We get caught up in the cycle of getting paid, paying others, and if there is anything left, well maybe we'll draw a wage. Instead why not set up on internet transfer that say $50 a week which goes into a 'Rainy Day' bank account. Don't touch it (unless absolutely critical) and it will build up. Remember also that if your trading entity is a company, ensure the savings account is also in the name of that entity, and not your personal name for example, so that the transfer is not considered wages.

Sales & Marketing

40 Get a database going from day one!
SALES & MARKETING

As soon as you start your business and start doing jobs, I strongly recommend you start capturing data. In fact, don't wait till you start a job, start this database as soon as you start getting enquiries and start quoting. You can do this in a number of ways, but possibly the simplest and easiest method would be an Excel spreadsheet, with the following fields:

First Name
Surname
Company (if they are a business)
Address line 1 (ie Unit 5)
Address line 2 (ie 12 Smith Street)
Suburb
State
Postcode
Mobile
Work Phone
Home Phone
Email address
Date of first contact
Details of quotes or work done

Now, with the above, I've got you splitting up first name from surname and not putting the complete address into one field. The reason is that if you want to convert to another system later (such as MailChimp or Infusionsoft) trust me, it will be SO much easier if you have formatted things well from day one.

Then when you get a contact, or do a quote or do a job, ensure that person is in your database. A good way to capture this info is to have those fields on your job sheets, so you remember to fill them out. The last field (details) will be much larger and could have numerous entries.

41 Market your business like a pro
SALES & MARKETING

So many tradies let the marketing and follow up not happen. So now you have a database – excellent! Use it. Keep in touch with your customers. Not just at Christmas, but regularly for an inspection or repair job. For example, electricians can have repeat work with air-conditioner services. Whether it be a service or check, you should be the one to remind your customers it's due – they frequently won't remember otherwise.

Also use your database for marketing or newsletters with tips and tricks in it. Engage your contacts to stay top of mind.

If you don't have the time to make the calls, hire someone to make calls and bookings for you – reminding your customers that a service is due, or that it's been 12 months since their last inspection. It costs any business 7-8 times more to get a new customer than to sell to an old one. If you rang your customers regularly and kept in touch, bet they would use you more. You will be 'top of mind'. Be pro-active, not reactive in getting work.

42 Don't put all your eggs into one basket!
SALES & MARKETING

You've heard this expression – we've all heard it heaps, and it's really important for anyone in the building game. So often these days, builders are going bust, large contractors declaring bankruptcy and guess who suffers? Well, it's frequently the tradie. You either get caught out not being paid a large chunk (potentially going under yourself) or you have lost a major source of income. Both scenarios are not good.

If you don't work solely for one person/builder/company, then you are less likely to be as badly affected in this scenario. Work for a few different people and then if work dries up with one, you work more with another. Personally, I recon three is the magic number here. Try to work for three different sources and whilst losing one of your builders might hurt, or if they don't pay you, it won't be enough to quite send you under.

Apply this same principle to your marketing as well! Don't simply just use a website, or advertise in the local paper and do nothing else. There are so many different options to market your business, so be sure to talk to your business coach or marketing consultant on all the options which are available.

Get more tips from this eBook. Email me at <u>donna@donna-stone.com.au</u> to get your copy now.

43 Turn up to quote!
SALES & MARKETING

This is a generalisation, and not the case all the time, but fact is that Tradies have a reputation - they are not reliable in turning up. In fact, one tradie based his business name on this concept and called himself "Always Turns Up Electrical" (now can't remember if he was electrical or plumbing – but you get the point). It's actually annoying as a consumer, because you can organise three quotes and you'll be lucky if even one turns up. Now I know in high times, this is the case, and certainly in an economic downturn, this is less often – but regardless of the economy you should be reliable and consistent. If you don't plan on turning up, then don't promise it.

44 Leave your card or fridge magnet
SALES & MARKETING

Don't assume your new customer will be able to find your number next time they need you. Give them your business card (or magnets are often better) so your number is super handy next time. And whilst you are there at any job, put a magnet or flyer in the mail box of the neighbouring properties either side of the job. People have likely seen your van/ute/truck with its signwriting on it at their neighbour's house – so there is a degree of familiarity. Leave your contact information with them, and a certain number will use you next time.

45 Follow up every quote!
SALES & MARKETING

Sorry to say, but tradies and builders are notoriously bad for not doing this. I remember a little while ago I had a fellow come around to give me a quote on my kitchen. I loved his work and happy with his price, but I'm a busy person. I waited three weeks for him to contact me to ask how the quote had gone but didn't hear from him. Eventually (after much searching) I found his quote and rang him. He was super keen to have the job, but had never thought about ringing me. Imagine I could not have found his card, or had I got a second quote and that person had rung me, I might have accepted their quote, simply because they rang and followed up and it was easy.

In business (and quoting) make it easy for people to do business with you. Provide a neatly written and clear quote. Include your terms and always follow up. Ring back in 24 to 72 hours and if they say "I've not had a chance to look at it properly" ask if you can follow up in a week and then diarise to do so.

Don't believe me? Then try it and see how much more work you pick up – simply because you picked up the phone after a quote. It can be simply saying "Hi, I'm Tom the Plumber and just wanted to check if you had any questions about that quote I left you Monday afternoon?" If they say they don't have questions, then ask for the business and say "So, would you like to book the job in?"

What have you got to lose? People don't mind a courtesy call and hey, you might pick up heaps of work!

46 Make the most of cheap advertising!
SALES & MARKETING

Your work vehicle is prime real estate for advertising. Use it!! Have your vehicle sign-written – it's amazing how many times I've been meaning to call a tradie, and I'm behind a ute for that trade, written down the number, or even rung there and then. It's easy and convenient – and when your vehicle is parked in a driveway, you are marketing your business, just by parking there.

47 Register for online lists/apps
SALES & MARKETNG

There are a good number of tradie services listings, both websites and now online apps – some you pay for and some are free. Search for your own trade and see what comes up and investigate whether you want to have a listing in this App or website.

48 Remember to upsell
SALES & MARKETING

The 'Golden Arches' do it so well "would you like fries with that?". So why don't you?   Did you know that if you ask a customer (whilst providing one service) if they would like a second service whilst you are there, statistically they will accept your offer 50% of the time!   Yes, half the time they will say 'yes'.   Whilst you're there, why not do a service, check the points, clean the filters, put in some energy efficient bulbs?   I'm sure you could think of a list of 'extras' you could do at most visits – and of course, ensure all your staff are trained up to do the same "up sell' offer.

49 Neat & tidy uniforms
SALES & MARKETING

Again, you may think that your personal presentation has zilch to do with the job you do. Maybe not, but the fact is that impressions do count. If you turn up to quote a job, in thongs, no uniform, long hair, piercings and a fag hanging out of your mouth – does this make a homeowner feel comfortable or confident? Some may have no concern whatsoever, but I can assure you that many others may feel very uncomfortable and may not even answer their door! Ensure that you and your staff:

- Are clean and neat. This does mean shaven, hair tidy and physically clean
- They don't stink – just because it's a hot day, doesn't mean your team need to stink - literally
- Wear a neat and professional uniform with the business name on it.
- Your team are respectful, speak politely and nicely.

Again, yes, you do need to do a good job; but it's all part of the customer service. Being professional doesn't mean you have to be a solicitor or accountant – tradies can be professional too!

50 Offer a guarantee
SALES & MARKETING

Guarantees do one critical thing. They remove the doubt and fear from dealing with a new person. It's called 'risk reversal'. If there is a written guarantee, then you believe and feel you have less to lose if they don't do what they said they would. Buying a product or service with a guarantee or warranty takes away some of that fear and doubt.

The reality is that you no doubt have an assumed guarantee in place; the fact is that if a customer came to you with a genuine problem you would fix it, rectify or replace. So what's stopping you from having a clear and assured guarantee?

Yes, I know there are some people who abuse guarantees. They complain purely from the hope of getting something for free. In fact, I'm sure some people make an occupation of it. However on the most part, most people don't claim on a guarantee. Give your guarantee thought, so it cannot be abused, or have systems in place, to be protected.

Lawyer's Tip

Goods and services that you supply to a consumer come with guarantees under Australian Consumer Law. These guarantees cannot be excluded and if breached the consumer is entitled to a remedy. Consumer guarantees apply to major and minor problems.

In addition to Australian Consumer Law you may also be required to give additional warranties to consumers under your licensing requirements.

A guarantee that goes above and beyond Australian Consumer Law and your licensing requirements may be great from a sales perspective, but it can be a nightmare from a liability and risk perspective - especially if you choose to write it yourself or borrow it from your competitors.

The risk is whether your guarantee is limited enough to protect you: are you going to be responsible for replacing the whole product forever, when your product has only a 7 year life span? What if the owner purposefully damages the product or someone else tries to repair it and instead breaks it?

Guarantees should always be written carefully and we recommend that they should always be written by a lawyer. You are committed to your guarantee for a long time, so make sure you can honour your guarantee without risking your business.

51 Get further education
SALES & MARKETING

I have written an e-book with a list of **OVER 200** lead generation tips, broken up into categories. This list is FREE on my website, just visit www.donna-stone.com.au. And if it happens to not be there, just email me and I'll send it to you – donna@donna-stone.com.au.

Remember the more ways you try to get business in and generate leads, the more business you are likely to have, and if you are doing things right, the greater your profit.

Operations

52 Plan your Week
OPERATIONS

So often our week gets away from us. By the time we work and quote and visit the sites, and drive from job to job and pay the wages, dang, we're exhausted. We find there are things we just didn't get time for, such as invoicing. So, I suggest you allocate certain times/days to activities.

It might be a case of getting up half an hour earlier to invoice, or perhaps you block out Wednesday mornings from 7am to 11am to invoice and do the office stuff. Whatever you do, I suggest you actually write it in your diary. So if the office is a Wednesday morning, put a line through that part of your diary "office" so you don't go and book a job, or agree to quote. I know you may feel that quoting or working is more important, but if you don't do the other things, such as invoicing, pretty soon you won't have the money to put fuel in your ute to go and quote!

53 Encourage an inspection prior to completion
OPERATIONS

You might consider client inspections along the way, and certainly after the completion of each stage. Having a client inspect the job, and better, sign off that they are happy really covers you for later. There are no excuses like "but that's not the colour I chose" or "it's 3 feet too far to the left". Being diligent now really does cover you. If a client signs off on work, let's say colour, then they can hardly come back later and say the colour is wrong. People change their minds, friends comment on the colour, or sometimes people are just looking for excuses to not pay you. Don't give them that opportunity.

54 Set formal inspection times
OPERATIONS

As a builder or renovator, it can often be a pain when the home owner decides to "inspect" the job site at random, without you and often during after hour periods. Not only is this a Workplace Health and Safety issue, but it also means you often cannot explain why something is as it is, or what's happening. You might be halfway through an activity, and they go into panic mode thinking it's all wrong. Or they ask one of your guys a question and the answer may not be the one you would have provided yourself. Eg "Yeah, that's a f***up but I guess the boss will fix it" - would not go down well.

May I suggest you organise regular inspection visits with your customers. Set a time to walk them through. Ensure the site is safe, warn your workers to be on their best behaviour, and have a clipboard on hand. Show them where things are at, answer questions AND if there is something which is not on track, better to rectify now whilst you are in the middle of it, rather than when the job is completely done. Open communication alleviates many possible problems and gives the home owner the opportunity to be kept informed, away from the site at other times, but also the chance to air any concerns. At this time, also have your Variation Book handy as well.

55 Face disputes front on and promptly
OPERATIONS

When we have a problem with something or a concern or complaint, what do we hate the most? That we cannot tell the relevant person what's bothering us. Being on hold for 20 minutes "you are progressing in the queue" or the manager avoiding our calls or the business owner not returning our calls – all adds fuel to the fire. Here's what to do:

- Ensure you (and your team) make yourselves available to listen immediately.
- Be sure to allow the person to speak. Let them finish speaking and avoid the urge to jump in and defend yourself.
- Once they've spoken, then firstly advise that you take the complaint seriously.
- Address their complaint. If you need time to speak to others and find out what's going on, then tell them this, but tell them you WILL come back to them.
- DO come back to them after your research.
- If you are in the wrong, admit this and apologise and advise them what you plan to do to rectify. Quite often, just having someone say "sorry" is the biggest thing.
- If you don't believe the complaint is reasonable, explain why. If you are able to give them something to keep them happy, that is your choice. Some people out there simply complain, without reason, to get a freebie. At least communicate with them.
- Finally, do what you promise. Ideally come back to the person, after rectification, and check they are happy.

Lawyer's Tip

> If a dispute arises you will need to be aware of the dispute procedures in your contract and your State's Security for Payment legislation (if relevant) because your options may be limited by strict time frames.
>
> Contact a local building and construction lawyer to help you through the dispute resolution process.

56 Quoting for Union jobs
OPERATIONS

If you are quoting for a Union job and not familiar with this, do take care. Union jobs can mean extra costs, expenses, rules and regulations. In fact, after you've investigated, you may decide it's not worth it, but at the very least you will take into account these extra costs when you cost out a job, so that you don't end up running the job at break-even, or worse, doing the job at a loss. One example is that you have to pay CIPQ and BEWT ... plus staff have to get a minimum level of super per week, even if they work only 4 hours – which may equate to be well above the current super guarantee level. Remember also the cost of being a Union Member, how working on a union site might affect your business. As always, as a business owner, you need to make an informed decision.

57 Workplace health & safety
OPERATIONS

Any large subcontractor or builder will be aware of WH&S requirements, particularly in respect of having a plan and your obligations. If you are a smaller tradie, you may or may not have to put in a formal Work Safety Plan (AKA Safe Work Method Statement). But you may, as I've found even the smaller tradie is getting caught up with having to provide this. But, even if you don't have a formal requirement, remember you do have an obligation of ensuring safety to both yourself, your team and those you work around, regardless of the size of your operation. On the most part, WH&S is common sense.

Do you leave electrical cords in water?
Do you allow items to drop from a height?
Do you leave sharp and jagged edges around where someone could cut themselves?

Of course, the answer is 'no' to all these. Simply use common sense. For example, over the years I cannot remember the number of times I've told my boys "Don't leave your skateboard in the corridor, someone will break their neck". Same concept applies – if you see something which may be dangerous, take action to ensure it doesn't become an incident.

If you are required to provide Work Plans, there are a number of great samples (often free) on the internet. Obviously you have to reword them to be applicable to your business and you, but on the most part they are there.

If you need help, just ask for it. Your industry body I am sure can guide you or I know a few experts in the field – just ask me for an introduction. Remember WH&S is a legal obligation and it's very important – please don't sweep it under the carpet.

58 Quoting … the overlooked costs
OPERATIONS

I've seen many quotes and job costs and what surprises me is how often overhead costs are overlooked. Overhead costs are things like your accounting bills, vehicle rego, bank interest, office wages, storage shed rental, just to name a few.

Most people, when they quote, will take into account their materials, labour and then add some profit and then add GST. The thing is that your overhead costs need to be accounted for. If, for example, these overhead costs equate to $180 per week. Say you usually just do one job per day (ie don't run multiple jobs at once). Let's say Job XYZ ran for one week. Let's say the profit (before overhead) was $150. Did you actually make a profit? The answer is no. Once you allow for your overhead costs of $180 per week, you actually lost $30. Keep this going week after week and you're running a business at a substantial loss.

59 Set time ranges for appointments
OPERATIONS

I know very well that jobs don't always run on schedule. You finish a job earlier, or another takes longer. It's really hard to turn up for appointments on time. So how about doing a little what Telstra or Foxtel do – have a time range. But rather than be totally open timed (say 7am to noon), make it an hour rate "we'll be there between 2:30pm and 3:30pm". Most people are fine with an hour time range, especially if they are just at home anyway. If the big boys can get away with insisting we sit at home several hours, I don't see a problem with 1 hour – it's just about communication.

60 Set days or times for special activities
OPERATIONS

I know a tradie one of my sons worked for – Monday is his admin/quoting/office day. You might choose a specific day or you might choose a time of day. Finish onsite at 3pm, do a quote on your way home and then spend an hour in the office before dinner. Think about what will work for you and try to be disciplined in those times. You can't please all the people all the time, but find what works for the majority. For some tradies, I know they devote Saturday morning for quotes as an alternative – but if you watch your kid's soccer on a Saturday, then that won't work for you.

61 Confirm via text that morning
OPERATIONS

Ever have problems with people not being at home for their appointment? Then confirm via text that morning. Usually most tradies work in pairs – so whilst one of you is driving, the other is confirming appointments via text. These days with smart phones, (and therefore larger keypads) there is less excuse to not text. Guys with even big fingers can text and if not, then have the apprentice next to you do it for you – who hopefully has smaller fingers. ☺

62 Clean up after yourself
OPERATIONS

Ok, I'm talking to you now as a woman – but it's a very common complaint. I get that you believe the most important part of the job is actually fixing the problem – whether it be a leaking loo or an electrical fault – but you know what the average householder remembers? They remember you turned up 3 hours late, left a huge mess and charged a fortune. Not that you did a fantastic job. So, please, understand how important it is for you to clean up the job after yourself. Take away the rubbish, the packaging boxes, sweep or vacuum the dust, sawdust or dirt and basically leave the job in a better state than when you arrived. I know you believe it's the job which is important, but believe me, it's often the little details that mean someone will keep your business card and call you again next time they need your service, or more importantly pass your number onto a friend or neighbour.

63 Don't Answer the Phone
OPERATIONS

It comes a time you simply need to turn it off so you can get the job finished. If you have an apprentice, let him (or her) babysit your phone. Give training on how to answer the phone and how to take a message, but it's better they are interrupted, than you who is worth so much more per hour. Yes, it may be a request for a job; so handle this in the process of training your assistant:

"Hi, Bob's Plumbing Services, this is Jason speaking. I'm sorry Bob is just fixing a customer's toilet at present, but I'll get him to call you back straight away. Can I grab your number please?" There are also phone answering services available, but test them; some are very stiff and flat and others provide an exceptional service.

64 Manage your Time!
OPERATIONS

Every business, regardless of the industry, struggles with time. We just don't have enough! Here are some obvious time stealers. Think about each of these and more important HOW you could avoid losing time in these areas.

I have written a whole e-book on Time Management (plus there is an audio) … see the next page, which includes heaps and heaps of practical ideas on how to save time. Check it out at http://www.donna-stone.com.au/.

Here's that list to get you thinking:

- Interruptions - telephone
- Interruptions - personal visitors
- Meetings
- Tasks you should have delegated
- Procrastination and indecision
- Perfectionism
- Acting with incomplete information
- Dealing with team members
- Crisis management (firefighting)
- Unclear communication
- Inadequate technical knowledge
- Unclear objectives and priorities
- Lack of planning
- Stress and fatigue
- Inability to say "No"
- Desk management and personal disorganisation

Remember this, do what you do well and outsource the rest. As a business coach I definitely work with clients to help them (and their staff) be more efficient with their time.

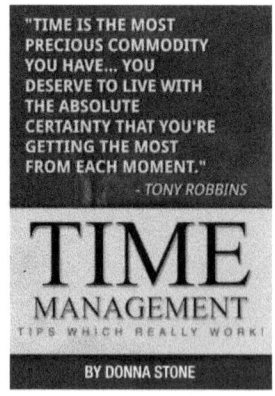

65 Work outside whilst the sun is shining!
OPERATIONS

Many tradies are affected by bad weather. So plan for this. Imagine you are a painter starting a new job. If the weather is great start outside and do the exterior painting, gutters, soffits, fences – all the external stuff first. Do the interior last. Because if you have a few wet days, you can easily move inside and continue work. However if you did all the interior work first, then you have to wait for the clouds to clear before you can finish your job.

66 Plan for seasonal ups and downs
OPERATIONS

With many businesses, we have seasonal ups and downs. If you are a lawn mower, then winter can be quiet. Same for pool cleaners. Some trades even close down for 4-6 weeks over Christmas. Firstly on a personal level, you really need to plan for having no income at this time. But if you are operating a business, think about what else you could do during your quiet spells. Here are some thoughts:

Lawn Mowing – how about tree pruning early spring? Or gutter cleaning in winter? Have a complimentary and associated business which can operate when your lawns are not growing.

Pool Maintenance – how about annual equipment testing for your regular customers?

Air conditioning/Electrical – test and clear air conditioners in winter when it's quieter – have specials for your customers to encourage them to give you work during the quiet times. Perhaps they get a value added service with every clean ... such as a safety inspection (if you are qualified).

These are just a couple of ideas; every industry has opportunities – it's just about putting on your thinking cap.

67 Balance your Life
OPERATIONS

On a final note for this chapter, it's best you find balance in your life. Ensure you eat well and get good exercise. If your health fails, then every likelihood so will your business. Remember why you go into business in the first place, and unless it was to ensure you worked every weekend, then don't. Slot in personal and family time too! You don't 'have' to work every weekend – you chose to. If you are super busy, consider alternatives.

Staff

68 Set up right to hire staff
STAFF

When you get to that point on hiring staff, you need to do it right. Your first dilemma is whether to put someone on as a contractor or employee. If the person is only working for you, they are doing regular hours, and really for all intents and purposes are an employee; I suggest you run them through payroll, pay super and include them in the relevant Workers Compensation policy.

Now I know you'll hear mates and do-gooders advising you to just put them on as a subbie. That way you don't have to pay Workers Compensation premiums or super. Not true. There are a number of criteria, but to keep it simple, I ask this question.

How is the person setup? What I mean by this is, are they operating as a sole trader, company, trust or partnership? If they are a sole trader, then you have a very hard time proving they are a true-blue contractor and should not be covered by super etc. I'm not saying it's impossible for a sole trader to be a contractor, but it's a hard one to prove. If the person really wants to be a contractor, then simply ensure they are a company, trust or partnership. The simple reason is that super and workers compensation cannot be paid to an entity, only an individual – i.e. sole trader. So if you are audited, the relevant officials will automatically not even look at a company, trust or partnership – only the sole traders.

And let me clarify a point. Sometimes people say they are a contractor because they have an ABN. Having an ABN doesn't make you a contractor and definitely does not mean you may not have to pay super or WorkCover for them. Their structure (company, trust etc) is one of the critical indicators.

Imagine you employ Bob Smith, who is a sole trader. Let's say the casual hourly rate is $30 per hour as an employee. Your workers compensation and super add on another roughly 15% ... so your true cost is $34.50. Now you may agree to pay Bob $35 per hour as a contractor, figuring you won't pay super or workers compensation. Let's say Bob works on average 40 hours a week. Over a year, that extra $5 an hour you pay him equates to an extra $10,000 per annum. Imagine you have 10 "Bobs". That's $100K. Now image you get audited all these "Bobs" are deemed workers and should have been covered.

Firstly, you're up for the cost of $100K in super and workers compensation. Then because you didn't pay on time, there are penalties, interest and fines. Then (this is the icing on the cake) the whole fine amount, including the base $100K may NOT be an allowable deduction (i.e. it's not a legit business expense which comes off your taxable income). Ouch!!! To say the least.

So in simple terms, unless someone is operating via a trust, company or partnership, then put them via wages and pay them super and cover them under your Workers Compensation policy – better safe than sorry.

Recruit the right person for the job
STAFF

So often it's tempting to just employ a mate, or your brother-in-law or that bloke who rocked up on site asking for work – simply because it's easy. Unfortunately the wrong employee will cost you a heap of money, often in being non-productive, or worse making mistakes that cost you in rectification. Statistically, the cost to replace staff is 2.5 x their salary. Think also about your reputation. If you have bad workers, chances are your regular customers or contractors will stop using you.

70 Know what you want
STAFF

If you are going to recruit yourself (check out my e-book called Recruitment & Retention on http://www.donna-stone.com.au) then be sure to be clear on what you want. Write it down as you may need to insert that in the job ad if it's an online job site. The local paper will allow for less space, so you can be clean, clear and precise.

71 Reference Check
STAFF

If you do nothing else, ring up their prior employers and ask questions about their work.   Don't be brief, really chat to the person and ask what their attitude was like, their workmanship and their reliability.   Why did they leave?   Would this person employ them again?

72 Test them out
STAFF

Ideally, put them on for a week's (paid) trial and see how they perform.   They will, of course, be on their best behaviour, but it will give you an idea of how they operate and perform.   Don't let emotion or feelings play on your decision to keep them or not. The fact they have four kids shouldn't affect your decision to not retain them, if they were absolutely hopeless at their job.

73 Have an Employment Agreement
STAFF

When you recruit for a position, you should have a list of duties that the position encompasses. Likewise, you should have a letter of appointment, or better yet, an Employment Agreement which outlines confidentiality, instant dismissal, pay conditions, accruals, benefits, rules, regulations etc. Ideally an Employment Agreement should be looked over by a solicitor, as it is a legal document. This document not only protects you, and your business but it actually protects your team.

If it is clear that staff cannot take your ideas and clients and set up in competition with you, then this protects both your business and the team you have working for you. If your business is protected, it is more likely to flourish and in return, your team are more likely to retain their jobs – so it's in everyone's best interest.

Lawyer's Tip

Like any contract, an employment contract must be in writing. To find out more about employment contracts, you can contact:

- Your local trade association
- Fair Work at www.fairwork.gov.au
- Your local employment lawyer.

74 While the cat is away, the mice will play!
STAFF

In any business this is the case, but it does seem to happen a lot in the trades. Now of course the cat is the boss and the mice are the staff. As you know, I've worked with building industry guys for decades and I've proven that most jobs run better when the boss is there. Both from an operational perspective and from a monetary angle. Now I know that there are some great supervisors out there, and in this case, the site supervisor is the boss really.

But when there is no strong supervisor and the business owner is absent, then frankly the guys (especially if they are being paid by the hour, and not per piece) can tend to slacken off (generally, and for those who do not, my apologies for the generalisation). I've seen it, the boss leaves the site, and tools are down and it's 'smoko' time. If you want your business to run effectively, then you need to have either:

- Great staff – you can trust
- Systems to ensure work is done
- A strong supervisor
- Don't leave the site long

SimPro (to mention one of many companies) offer a range of products and services or tracking projects, GPS monitoring of vehicles and for very large trucks there is IVMS (In Vehicle Monitoring Systems). If you are able to track vehicles, it's great to know where the vehicles are in order to improve efficiency.

75 Obey the Rules
STAFF

I'm going to keep this short. There are certain things you **have** to do:

- Provide a safe workplace and document it's a safe workplace. There are so many plans and information on the website, just make sure you keep your team safe.

- Not allow bullying to occur. Whether it's you calling your apprentice a "Dumb $%&%W#" or one of your staff calling another a derogatory name based on his ethnic background, this is all illegal. Hey, you can't even wolf whistle a lady walking past the job. (I sort of miss that one a little).

- Pay them super – unless they are a genuine contractor, don't try to avoid paying their super – the fines and penalties are just not worth it.

- Cover them for Workers Compensation – again unless they are a genuine contractor. And on that point I would also stipulate that they are structured properly, ie a company or trust, otherwise do the super and work cover.

- You need to be an equal opportunity employer; so you can't dismiss an applicant for a position due to their religion, gender, race, age or sexual preference, although obviously age or gender may negate some people due to their physical abilities – be sensible about it, but also be careful of what you say.

- Take complaints from your workers seriously; these days it's so easy for them to lodge an official complaint and you'll be in deep trouble.

76 Use apps for timesheets
STAFF

There are now some great Apps (free and small priced) which are great for staff to track their time in a timesheet format on their smart phone and then email over to the office at the end of the week. Whilst there are a few, one I know about is Timesheet Pro. Use technology to make your life easier!

77 Use videos for training purposes
STAFF

Sick of saying the same thing over and over again? Not really a typist and want to type up instructions for your team? Here is a great idea for you then!

Often watching a video on how something is to be done is far better than reading a thick manual, where you just find yourself fading out after the first 20 minutes. Doing a video is like a template – you do it once and then won't have to do again for quite some time. It saves you actually having to personally train new staff yourself ever again. The video is actually something like a clone, which means you can get on with your business and allow the video to train and induct your staff. Remember, if you have a larger organisation, then this really is an excellent option. The one drawback I see is the edits can be difficult to action. It can easily be done on most smart phones.

Glossary of Terms

(Accounting)

Assets – these are things that you own. They are balance sheet accounts which include things like money in the bank, or buildings, or your motor vehicles, tools and equipment. The opposite are liabilities.

Asset Purchases - yes a legal business expense, or deduction, but legally (as with all the above examples) this also gets coded to the balance sheet, as an asset. It's referred to as "capitalising" an expense. So again, you may spend a heap of money buying assets, which will not show in your P&L as an expense. Either at month end, or year end, the bookkeeper or accountant will journal in the depreciation for the asset. It's only the depreciation which is deductible.

Balance Sheet – this is a statement of your equity and essentially a listing of a everything you own, less everything that you owe. The net result is your equity.

Cost of Goods Sold (COGS) - also known as Direct Costs. These are the costs directly relating to making income. They are such things as subbies, materials, site setup fees, equipment hire for a site (porta loo, crane hire etc). The best way to work out if a cost is direct or indirect (overhead) is that direct costs only exist if you are doing work and selling. If you didn't work for 6 months, then you shouldn't be purchasing materials or paying subbies but you might still be paying your phone bill, or paying your accounting for your tax preparation.

Creditors - the other side of the coin. When you purchase business expenses on credit, you owe the money. If you record the expense in your accounting software as a purchase, then you will have recorded the expense, but until you pay the supplier, it sits as a credit on your balance sheet.

Debtors - this is the money owed to you. So when you sell $100 (ex GST) to a customer on credit, it will show as income in your P&L until that customer pays their bill. That it sits in an asset account called "Trade Debtors". This is one critical reason that businesses often see great profit (due to good sales) but cannot understand why their cash-flow is rubbish – the sale hasn't been collected yet! The money is sitting in the balance sheet as a debtor, not as cash in bank.

Drawings – these are the owners' personal expenses. They are NOT a business deduction and so should not be coded to the P&L and in fact instead go usually on the balance sheet to a liability account often called Directors Loan Account (if it's a company) OR if you're a partnership or sole trader it might be an equity account called "Owners Drawings".

Liability - these are something that you owe. It's a debt, such as a BAS debt, or loan, or HP or your creditors. These are balance sheet accounts.

Loans, HP's & Finance - often when you pay a loan or HP or chattel mortgage, you code the payment to the liability account. So although it's often a business expense, the expense doesn't actually get posted to the P&L statement until the point when the interest component is claimed. Now this might be done monthly but a profession bookkeeper who has gained the capital/interest split, OR by the accountant at year end. So if you pay heaps in vehicle finance or other loans, your actual P&L statement may not yet reflect this.

Overhead Expenses - these are the expenses which relate to you doing business and are not direct costs. Examples are accounting fees, bank charges, motor vehicle rego, licenses and telephone costs.

Profit & Loss Statement - this is a listing of all your income, less all your expenses. The bottom line or balance is essentially your profit. It's often known as a P&L.

Found this book useful and could make use of some help with support, guidance and accountability?

I offer services around Coaching, Mentoring, Training or Consulting on:

* Business Plans, Goal Setting & Strategy
* Marketing, Sales & Perception
* Staff Recruitment & Retention
* Finances & Profit Growth
* Systems & Procedures
* Time & Efficiency

Please contact me directly on 0411 622 666 or donna@donna-stone.com.au to discuss your needs.

114

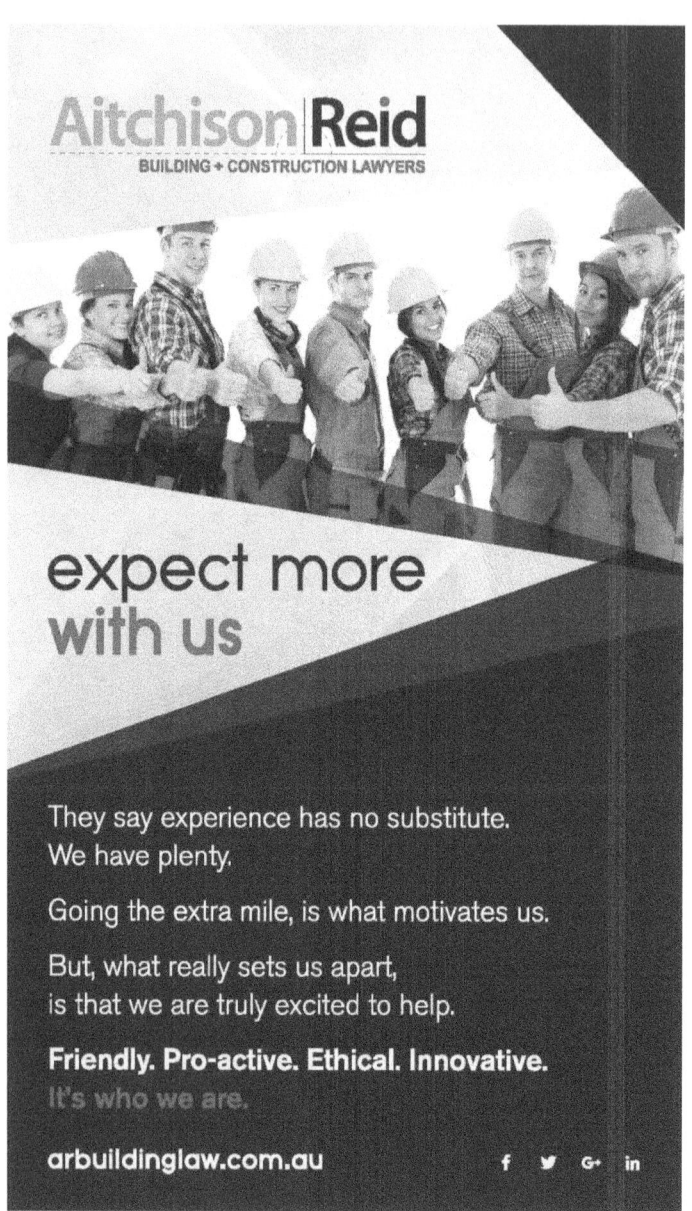

WHY AITCHISON REID?

We are a building and construction law practice, which means we are completely focussed on the law relating to your industry.

We predominately act for sub-contractors and trade contractors, just like you. So we understand the risks and issues that relate to your business.

We see ourselves as part of the construction industry rather than a law firm that just happens to do construction law work.

This means:

• We are friendly and approachable;

• Our offices are in an industrial estate and not in the city;

• We provide workshops that help educate subcontractors and trade contractors in the industry; and

• We are actively involved in the construction industry whether through support groups (such as Women in Building and Construction and NAWIC) or attending consultation meetings and making submissions on new legislation.

WHAT WE DO

We have plenty of experience helping contractors just like you with their disputes. We can help you with your disputes, whether it is:

• A debt due;

• Court proceedings (All courts and QCAT);

• An adjudication through the Building and Construction Industry Payments Act 2004;

• A subcontractor's charge;

• A mediation;

• An expert determination; and

• An arbitration.

But, we would we like to work with you before any disputes occur. We want to help you increase the chances of getting paid and to put you in the best possible position if a dispute occurs. We can do this by:

• Reviewing your business processes, and the contracts and subcontracts that you have been given for jobs you're tendering for or have won; and

• Drafting contracts personalised to your business.

Let's face it, the construction industry is often a hard place to run a business with tight margins and cashflow, so let us work with you to make it easier.

Stepping Stones to Business Success
Stepping Stones to Business Growth
Stepping Stones to Business Excellence

Order your copies now by visiting:

www.donna-stone.com.au

or call 1800 77 65 61

Pay via Visa, MasterCard, Cheque, Direct Deposit or PayPal

Special rates for bulk orders

www.ingramcontent.com/pod-product-compliance
Lightning Source LLC
Chambersburg PA
CBHW070040210526
45170CB00012B/545